Consumer Focused Behavior

Business Case Studies

Fred Santino

Fred Santino

Fred Santino
P.O. Box 214
North Chelmsford, MA 01863
fredsant27@outlook.com
Consumer Focused Behavior – Business Case Studies,
Fred Santino, First Printed Edition 2024
ISBN: 979-8-218-50169-3

Dedication

This book is dedicated to my wife, Ruth-Ann, who was an incredible mom to our two sons and enlivened every day until her unfortunate passing. Finally, I dedicate this to all those who served their country, particularly those who did not make it back.

Fred Santino

Acknowledgements

This book would not have been possible without the help of Debby, my good friend and dance instructor. A published author herself, Debby not only encouraged and inspired me to write, but also guided me through the process. My research for this book has spanned over the past twenty-years that I have been teaching at Boston University, plus the five years that I taught at Babson College. I also appreciate the suggestions that I received from the Chelmsford, MA Writers Group.

Fred Santino

Table of Contents

Fred Santino

Preface

Succeeding in business does not usually require creation of some novel idea, instead it requires being aware of customer needs and/or gaps in the market. A successful business finds a way to be aware of consumer behavior trends, such as a shift in preferences, declining or increasing popularity, and identifying the customers' problems or "pain." In this book, I have identified many situations to which businesses have responded to customer trends and feedback and adapted successfully. There also are situations where businesses have been unsuccessful, by misinterpreting or ignoring feedback, or being totally unaware of consumer trends.

Fred Santino

Chapter One
Automotive Consumer Behavior

Toyota is one of the world's top-selling and most reliable automakers. Japanese automaker Toyota is concentrating its efforts to offer cars people really want to buy. Toyota is proudly lagging in marketing all-electric vehicles. While rivals like General Motors, Kia, and Hyundai are offering out a variety of different electric vehicles for American consumers, Toyota is offering only one electric vehicle, the bZ4X crossover SUV.

During January 2024, Toyota chairman Akio Toyoda explained why his company has hesitated to invest in electric vehicles. Toyoda predicted that BEVs (battery-electric vehicles) would only capture a maximum of thirty percent of the automotive market share, since the BEVs require infrastructure that is not accessible to many customers.

The Chairman predicted that the other seventy percent of the market would consist of hybrids, fuel cell electric vehicles, hydrogen-powered cars, and traditional engine-powered cars.

According to Kelley Blue Book, over 1.2 million EVs hit the streets in 2023, representing just a seven percent market share. Though EV sales are slowing down compared to years prior, Toyota is planning a massive attack on the electrified car segment. Toyota, known for the Prius and hybrid versions of popular models like the Corolla and RAV4, is planning to turn most, of its gasoline-powered models into hybrids. Toyota's preference for hybrids over EVs is a challenge to government officials and the auto industry, which believe that all cars of the future will be electric.

Already, most of Toyota's lineup is either a hybrid or can be ordered with a powertrain. With this plan in place, Toyota must determine whether it wants to continue to sell non-hybrid versions of its cars. "Going forward, we plan to evaluate, car line by car line, whether going all-hybrid makes sense," Christ told Reuters. One target for being hybrid-only is the RAV4 crossover SUV. According to data from Kelley Blue Book, the RAV4 is the top-selling Toyota model and was the fourth best-selling car last year, moving nearly a half-million units to driveways across the nation.

The RAV4 is due for a major makeover for the 2026 model year. People familiar with Toyota's product planning said that the automaker will probably make the crossover solely a hybrid in North America. For the 2025 model year, Toyota has made a controversial decision to convert the very popular Camry sedan to solely a solely hybrid powertrain.

Toyota's strategy of making hybrid powertrains the sole engine choice for gas-powered cars aims to strengthen its position in a market that is seeing a comeback amid slowing EV sales.

While EVs need to be charged at charging stations, hybrids like the Toyota Prius can be filled up at any nearby gas station. The Prius' has outstanding mileage up to 57 miles per gallon, which allow for less frequent trips to the gas station. This also keeps the Toyota brand in compliance with EPA carbon-emissions regulations.

Toyota's hybrids are a well-developed technology with few, if any, risks. Toyota's approach of favoring hybrids makes things easy for the public who do not have to change their lifestyle. An electric vehicle is a disruptive technology, requiring massive change by the consumer, and development of infrastructure to support the technology. Not every consumer wants to change for little of no personal benefit.

Toyota executives explained that its hesitation toward EVs is also based on the limited amount of critical resources like lithium, cobalt, nickel and graphite

Fred Santino

Toyota Camry 2024 (PD)

Toyota Prius 2024 (PD)

Consumer Focused Behavior

According to Toyota, the automaker is making a huge commitment to gas-powered hybrid vehicles with consumer behavior in mind. These gas-powered hybrids, as well as gas-only autos and trucks are the vehicles that most people have expressed a preference for. Toyota hopes that customers will decide the outcome of the vehicle market, not arbitrary regulatory direction or political pressure.

Fred Santino

Chevrolet Malibu 2024 (PD)

Cadillac CT4 Sedan 2024 (PD)

Consumer Focused Behavior

Consumer Preferences: SUV's vs. Sedans

Sedans had started to decline in popularity around 2004. Besides more room, one of the most significant factors that lead the shift from sedans to SUVs and crossovers was safety features. SUVs and crossovers are typically larger and heavier than sedans, which can provide more protection in the event of a collision.

Car makers also were responsible for the shift. In 2016, Stellantis, the maker of Dodge and Chrysler declared that they would stop making sedans. Ford stopped producing sedans for the U.S. market in 2018. In May 2024, General Motors announced that it would end production of the Chevrolet Malibu, which was first introduced in 1964. GM's ending production of the Chevy Malibu is the latest action that the Big Three automakers are abandoning the U.S. sedan market.

The shift from sedans toward SUV's and trucks leaves Americans without affordable choices. The Malibu, with its MSRP starting at $25,100, has been one of the most affordable domestic-produced cars, costing half as much as the average new vehicle, costing $47,000. The Malibu is also a few thousand dollars cheaper than the Bolt that will replace it at the Kansas factory.

Consumers are not rushing to buy expensive SUV's in response to carmakers elimination of sedans. Sedans are still alive, and the Toyota Camry proves that. Camry is the best-selling sedan in America, proving more popular than notable SUVs like the Jeep Grand Cherokee, Chevrolet Equinox, and Ford Explorer. Sales were nearly stagnant in 2023, though, dropping slightly by 1.5 percent. Tesla offers two sedans: the Model 3 and Model S, and GM's Cadillac division will continue to offer two luxury sedan models. Sedans are marking a slight increase after years of decline.

The latest data from Q1 2023 shows that sedans and other types of cars made up 21.4 percent of the 3.6 million new vehicles sold, up from 19.6 percent in Q4 2021, marking a slight increase after years of decline. This shift is noteworthy since the share of cars has been on the decline in the U.S. since 2002.

Automotive News reported that, remarkably, sales of sedans, coupes, hatchbacks, convertibles, and sports cars increased in 2023. They are nowhere near matching SUV's, but they are on the rise.

Industry experts believe that some people will always prefer a sedan over a crossover or SUV. There is also a growing portion of younger people who, like their ancestors before them, don't want to drive the same sort of vehicle that their parents did.

Although the Malibu was not exactly a "dazzling" vehicle, GM produced 10 million of them, over the past 60 years. With a price starting at a relatively affordable $25,100, Malibu sales exceeded 130,000 vehicles in 2023, a 13 percent annual increase and enough to rank as the number three Chevy model, behind only the Silverado and the Equinox. That was not enough to keep the Malibu in production. The company says that the last Malibu will come out of its Kansas City, KS, factory this November; the plant will then be retooled to produce the new Chevy Bolt, an electric crossover SUV. With the Malibu's ending, GM will no longer sell any affordable sedans in the U.S.

As recently as 2009, U.S. passenger cars (including sedans and a plunging number of station wagons) outsold light trucks (SUVs, pickups, and minivans), but today they are less than 20 percent of new car purchases. That decision is bad news for road users, the environment, and budget-conscious consumers—and it may ultimately come around to bite Detroit.

When asked, automakers are quick to blame the sedan's decline on shifting consumer preferences. Americans simply want bigger cars, the story goes, and there is some truth to it. Compared to sedans, many SUV and pickup models provide extra cargo space and give the driver more visibility on the highway. In a crash, those inside a heavier car have a better chance of escaping without injury—although the same cannot be said for pedestrians or those in other vehicles.

Federal policy has distorted the car market to favor larger vehicles. Fuel economy regulations, for instance, are more lenient for SUVs and pickups than they are for smaller cars, nudging automakers to produce more of the SUV's and fewer of the smaller cars. Another factor is that small business owners, such as real estate agents, can save thousands of dollars by writing off the cost of their vehicle—but only if it weighs more than 6,000 pounds, a stipulation that entirely excludes sedans.

Carmakers influence consumer demand through billions of dollars spent on advertising. Because SUV's and pickups are more expensive and profitable than sedans, manufacturers have a clear incentive to promote those vehicles and encourage shifting away from small cars and toward larger ones. This explains why ad campaigns are designed to show off the benefits of SUV's.

Even those who do not want a big car may feel pressure to buy one, to avoid being at a disadvantage in a crash, or sitting higher to see what is ahead on the road. Many people find themselves in a dilemma, preferring smaller cars, but resigning themselves to buying an SUV since others already have them.

For all these reasons, modest-size sedans like the Malibu are disappearing from American streets, supplanted by SUV's and that seem to grow larger with every new model year.

The decline of the sedan is bad news for road safety. The U.S. underperforms in road safety compared to the other nations, especially for bicyclists and pedestrians. Larger cars have bigger blind spots, convey more force in a collision, and tend to strike a person's torso rather than their legs. They are also heavier, with propulsion systems that guzzle more gasoline to move, producing more pollution in the process. Their weight causes the erosion of tires and roads, scattering particles that can damage human health as well as the environment.

Despite the myriad problems of large cars, the federal government has taken no steps to restrain it. In the absence of regulations or taxes, carmakers have ample reason to abandon their sedan models in favor of SUV's and trucks. The higher margins of larger cars is especially valuable now, as the Big Three automakers need funds to invest in newer technology, and pay for the rising employees' wages and benefits.

It may be a difficult task to pivot back to selling small cars, even if the American auto industry wanted to. They have lost their expertise and infrastructure to produce cheaper small cars in high volumes.

The shift from sedans toward SUVs and trucks leaves everyday Americans with a strained wallet. With its MSRP starting at $25,100 the Malibu has been one of the most affordable U.S.-produced cars, costing barely half as much as the average new vehicle, which exceeded $47,000 recently.

Especially when factoring in higher interest rates and spiking insurance premiums, cars are becoming a financial strain for many Americans. According to the Federal Bureau of

Transportation Statistics, the average annual, inflation-adjusted cost of owning a vehicle and driving it 15,000 miles hit $12,182 in 2023, an increase of over 30 percent in just six years.

If consumer preferences shift away from the larger SUV's, the lack of sedan production leaves the Big Three automakers vulnerable to foreign automakers which are still selling lots of sedans. With end of Malibu production, Detroit has abandoned the last affordable sedan, at least for now. This seems to indicate a lack of long-term thinking. Having fewer models may make for efficient manufacturing, but it ignores consumer behavior and a large segment of potential customers. The automakers may regret their decision later. (Source #1, 2)

Consumer Focused Behavior

Acura sedan 2024 (PD)

Fred Santino

Sweetgreen interior (PD)

Chapter Two
Fast Casual Dining and Customers

S weetgreen, an "upscale" innovative salad chain used an awareness of consumer behavior and customer needs to achieve success. Sweetgreen stores are primarily located in urban areas like Boston, MA. or Los Angeles, CA. Sweetgreen, offers everything a health-conscious millennial might want, including a constantly changing selection of fresh food, a community feel in its stores, and a social media presence. Sweetgreen used customer data information to design retail stores and mobile apps. Sweetgreen's mobile app brings together online ordering, payment and Sweetgreen rewards, allowing customer to easily obtain their healthy farm-to-table fare. The customer can select their salad components while calculating nutritional and caloric information. Sweetgreen's app lets you reorder your favorites with just five clicks and order transportation to pick up your salad. Most important, the app shortens the waiting line. Sweetgreen designs their stores to serve as community hubs for interpersonal contacts. The store's music and art is selected to complement the food and enhances the dining experience.

Fred Santino

Sweetgreen is transparent about their food supply chain, and in-store operation. They list their produce sources in each location. Also, Sweetgreen's open kitchen design lets customers see the fresh produce coming into the kitchen and being prepared for customers. Sweetgreen described their development process, "We used data simulation and modeling to layout new Sweetgreen locations for efficiency and customer throughput. That leads to shorter waits and seamless online-order pickup. It's our mission. We build healthier communities. Optimizing our operations and capacity helps us do just that."

Sweetgreen's app identifies items that are in season at each store. In 2016, Sweetgreen unveiled an ordering app that lets users both customize orders and count calories. The display features 60 different ingredients and is compatible with the Apple Health app. The food is served as quickly as "fast food," but with complete nutritional information. With this technology consumers have one less excuse to eat unhealthy food.

In 2016, Sweetgreen announced that it would only accept credit and debit cards. Cashless policies had become popular in several cities, with some business owners saying that handling cash is inefficient and invites theft. One advantage of a cashless system is safety. Having no cash results in fewer robberies which threaten employees. Another advantage is health since many dollars and coins, which pass from hand to hand, have germs and not something you want people touching your food to be contacted with. The greatest advantage to a cashless operation, is speed of payment. Transactions are much faster when customers use a credit card or their phone. The no-cash policy helped reduce the waiting lines at busier times. When Sweetgreen was cashless, their revenue was not affected. Even the fees charged by credit cards were outweighed by the advantages.

Sweetgreen was praised as the example of a cashless success story, but that was short-lived. Sweetgreen's cashless policy raised issues about excluding certain groups of people— particularly seniors or low-income people. It discriminated against the lowest income earners who rely on cash. The company was trying to find an innovative a solution to accommodate such customers, but customers "left out" took to the courts.

There was a rising backlash to Sweetgreen's cashless policy. In 2019, Philadelphia, PA passed a law requiring most retail establishments to accept cash. This made Philadelphia the first U.S. city to ban stores and restaurants from implementing cashless policies. Business owners who did not comply faced fines of up to $2,000. Massachusetts followed by passing a similar law to allow Sweetgreen customers the right to pay cash at their Boston area locations. In a turn of events and an admission of defeat, the restaurant publicly admitted that its cashless experiment failed because it unfairly discriminated against those who did not have credit cards for whatever reason. Finally, in 2019, Sweetgreen announced it would accept cash payments nationwide, less than three years after implementing their cashless policy.

Recently, Amazon learned the same lesson, announcing plans to accept cash in their new Amazon Go shops. In the US, cash is still the most frequently used payment form. The Federal Reserve shows that 30 percent of all transactions and 55 percent of transactions under ten dollars are cash. Even with online shopping seemingly the norm, 77 percent of payments are still made in person.

Consumer Focused Behavior

Sweetgreen bowls (PD)

Sweetgreen has devoted a lot of its resources to digital technology and constant innovation. In 2018, it announced a new and partnership with a company, Row Seven, to use innovative technology when sourcing ingredients. They used the very latest in agricultural technology to develop a new type of squash to create a new breed of the squash which was then used in two brand-new Sweetgreen recipes.

During the Covid-19 pandemic with many offices closed, Sweetgreen was affected by fewer workers going into the office. Since the end of the pandemic, Sweetgreen's research identified that more people were working remotely, and that more consumers wanted to order food online with "contactless" pickup. Sweetgreen sought a new way to lure in the lunch crowd, offering the most upscale salad for a premium price. Sweetgreen's menu was intended to attract those workers who forgot to pack lunch or were working remotely.

To appeal to a broader array of customers, the company announced that it planned to pilot a drive-in concept in Highlands Ranch, Colorado. Calling it an "updated, healthy version of the traditional drive-thru," Sweetgreen said the drive-in will feature technology-enabled ordering as well as an innovative design. The Sweetgreen drive-in will feature a drive-thru lane for customers who ordered food from the Sweetgreen app, ahead of time, to pick up their food and go. Others can park and order via the chain's in-car ordering process. Guests will also be able to dine at the restaurant's outdoor patio. Sweetgreen says that these innovations will deliver on its mission of "connecting people to real food to life."

Fred Santino

Panera exterior (PD)

Panera Pick-Two meals (PD)

Panera Bread Not Paying Attention to Consumers

In evaluating a restaurant, food must be good, but it is not as important as the service to provide the food. Panera's service is very impersonal and involves waiting in lines, which makes a bad impression. Based on recent samples of customer feedback, Panera's customers would be happier if a server could bring the food to your table. Servers could get tips possibly making them more customer focused. Service is not something that can be "stockpiled" since the service is created and delivered at each time of purchase.

Panera Bread's menu is very confusing, with way too many choices. A few basic salads with a choice of toppings would be easier for the customer to order. The same goes for their sandwiches. The menu often seems different than the food they serve you.

The kitchen area looks empty, because nearly everything comes to the restaurant with minimal work necessary to prepare the food for customers. There are no chefs in the back, and even the bakers have only minimum tasks. Since many Panera items come to the store premade, it is not surprising that many consumers just buy those Panera items, such as soup, at the grocery store and eat less costly at home. Despite Panera's promotion of a "clean menu," some of its menu items are not as healthy as they once were.

Fred Santino

One noticeable thing about the Panera Bread menu is that the bagel texture is different from traditional bagels. The difference is because Panera does not use boiling, the traditional way to make bagels. Boiling provides an obvious chewy interior. However, Panera opting to steam the bagels rather than boil them. The resulting bagels are more like bread, which can be disappointing for customers wanting a New York-style bagel.

In 2015, Panera started changing its menu, vowing not to use a list of artificial ingredients, Panera defines "clean" foods as having no "artificial preservatives, sweeteners, flavors, and colors." This can be incorrectly perceived that everything on the menu is healthy, but nutrition is questionable. When looking at Panera's nutritional information, its Macaroni and Cheese bread bowl has the most calories (1,150) and the most carbs (164 grams). A large bowl of Macaroni and Cheese has 64 grams of fat and 35 grams of saturated fat. When it comes to sodium, the Chicken Cordon Bleu Melt on a baguette is its worst offender, clocking in at 3,510 milligrams of sodium. It and other Panera menu items exceed the daily sodium recommendation of 2,300 milligrams. The pastries are not as sugary as the drinks, with a 30-ounce Tropical Punch has 112 grams of sugar.

Consumer Focused Behavior

Bakery worker (PD)

Fred Santino

Glyphosate is an herbicide on their crops to kill weeds. When chain restaurants were tested for glyphosate in 2019, the amount found in the food at Panera was at levels that could potentially lead to health problems.

There are no chefs in the kitchen making Panera's soups or the macaroni and cheese from scratch. Boxes of pre-packaged soups and/or macaroni and cheese arrive at the restaurant frozen into giant bricks. An employee thaws and heats the frozen bricks in a hot water bath using a thermal oven before pouring them into serving pans. Panera's cooking seems like "heating up military rations." Also, the soup that being served may not be today's soup. Leftover soup is stored overnight if plastic bags sinks filled with ice. The first people ordering soup on any given day, could be eating yesterday's leftover soup.

Panera bakers do not make bread from scratch. A third party makes the dough and ships it to the restaurant frozen, however, it is still baked fresh on-site every day. Some locations replenish stock with newly baked items throughout the day. However, others only restock at the beginning of the day.

Panera has been criticized for the caffeine level of its Charged Lemonades. A 20-ounce drink has 156 milligrams of caffeine, while a 30-ounce drink has 234 milligrams, the equivalent of two and a third cups of coffee, or seven cans of Coca-Cola. Customers did not realize the drink had such high levels of caffeine. A Florida man with high blood pressure died in 2023 after drinking three Charged Lemonades. In May 2024, Panera removed the beverage from its menu.

Panera's menu offers the same items for different prices, depending how you order. Value Duets are cheaper than ordering off the You Pick Two menu. The Value Duets are a single price, while the You Pick Two menu allows you to pick two items from the varied menu, either ½ size or full size, and you can get a free side.

Panera's standards have lowered in recent years. They no longer show "antibiotic-free, hormone-free, vegetarian-fed, grass-fed, or pasture-raised animals." Healthier products are more expensive or unavailable. Using confined chickens again will save Panera $29 million. Panera described their plans, "We are focused on serving food our guests can feel good about, with the right combination of quality, taste, and value. As we grow to reach more guests, we continue to hold ourselves to high standards of quality for the ingredients we use." (Source #5, 12)

Fred Santino

Subway sandwich (PD)

Chapter Three
Sandwich Shops and Consumers

In recent years, prices at the Subway sandwich chain have jumped drastically. Footlong submarine sandwiches are priced now at $14-15 and six-inch submarine sandwiches are priced now around $10. The increased prices caused Subway to lose customers to rivals like Firehouse Subs, Jimmy John's and Jersey Mike's. According to financial data, Subway stores had been less profitable than its three main competitors, Jersey Mike's, Firehouse Subs and Jimmy John's, all of which take in about $1 million per unit, with an average Subway location taking in less than $500,000. Subway had been struggling, and thousands of Subway stores have closed since 2016. Subway had to change to keep present customers and get new customers. In an increasingly customer-centric world, companies that fail to adapt to customer needs run the risk of disappearing.

Subway made several changes to better appeal to consumers, including in 2023, Subway revamped its menu, adding more nutritious options like premium meats, plant-based alternatives, and locally sourced produce. In 2023, Subway introduced freshly sliced meat, which was a major shift from Subway's previous method of having the meat sliced at its factories before being delivered to its stores.

Fred Santino

After pressure from franchise owners, Subway kicked off its largest initiative to bring customers back. Stores received massive makeovers, with brighter lighting, sleeker furniture, vegetable displays, digital menu boards, and improved seating. In 2016, Subway replaced its logo with a brighter, cleaner look to adapt to changing customer demands. A year later, they redesigned the menu to offer pre-made creations rather than customizations. They also put out a more neatly organized menu board, with numbers and new names to speed up service

In 2024, Subway introduced "Subway Sidekicks," a new menu category. They also introduced "signature wraps" on lavash-style flatbread. Subway is also introducing a new rewards program giving discounts as customers spend more. Customers also get surprises, including free cookies and chips.

Despite Subway's changes, fewer customers are patronizing Subway's stores, and stores are continuing to close.

(Source #3, 16)

Consumer Focused Behavior

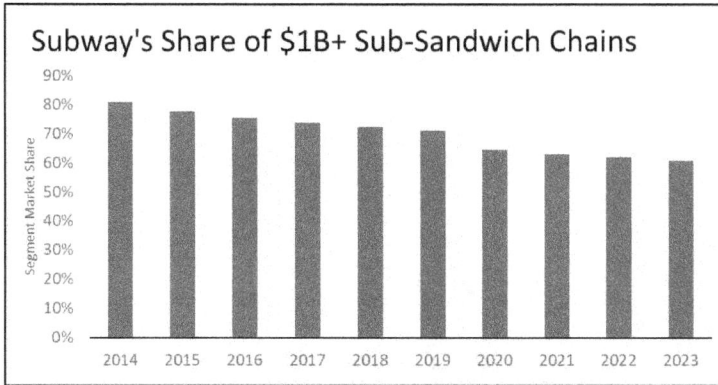

Subway's Share of $1B+ Sub-Sandwich Chains

(Source – Restaurant Research, Charlotte, NC)

Fred Santino

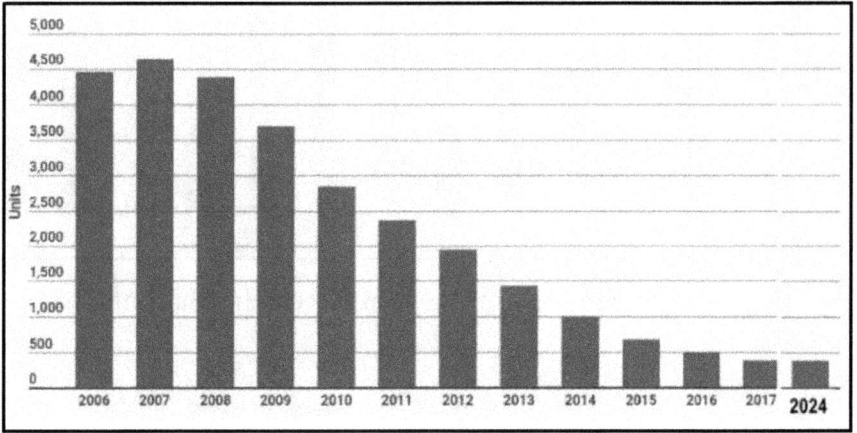

Decline of Quiznos stores 2006-2024
(Source: Franchise City, Toronto, CA)

Quiznos - sandwich chain collapses

Quiznos, the once high-growth sandwich chain, went from having 4700 shops to the present 148 remaining shops. Quiznos' recent customer reviews of 1.8 out of 5, show that most customers were dissatisfied with food quality and lack of service.

Quiznos is an example of what happens when a restaurant owner does not understand the needs, wants, and behavior of its potential customers. Quiznos is also an example of what happens to customers when a franchise operator does not provide adequate support for its franchisees.

Promotional campaigns are very important for any business, but the campaign must have some relation to the consumer behavior of their target customers. In February 2004, Quiznos ran an advertising campaign titled "Spongemonkeys" that was so unpopular that some franchisees posted signs apologizing for them, and saying they had nothing to do with the weird campaign. In the first week, Quiznos' Denver headquarters received 30,000 phone calls from people complaining about the ad campaign. Quiznos ended the ad campaign by August, but it had already brought a negative image to their business. Quiznos could not explain how the ad campaign was related to their customer base. Business Insider called Quiznos' "Spongemonkeys" advertising campaign "creepy" and "One of The 10 Worst Ad Campaigns Of All Time," and customers agreed.

In 2009, Quiznos corporate offered coupons for free sandwiches with hopes of getting people in their doors again. This attracted lots of customer attention, and visits to Quiznos' stores. Soon, the news media was reporting that customers were being denied their free sandwiches. Some locations did not honor the coupons at all, others only accepted them if customers bought something else. Customers got very angry. The franchisees had a very good reason for refusing to accept the coupons they weren't being compensated by corporate, and instead were expected to eat the cost of the "free" subs. At the same time, Subway was offering their "footlong" sandwich for $5.00. Part of Subway's success was their relatively lower prices, which Quiznos was unable to compete with. Subway was offering affordable prices, while Quiznos was offering higher prices. With Americans suffering through economic difficulties, the lower-priced store was an easy choice. Quiznos' free sandwich fiasco came just as the 2009 recession hit. The recession was bad on the restaurant industry, as consumers cut back on dining out, and Quiznos felt the decline.

Quiznos did not treat its franchisees fairly seemed to ignore how their treatment of franchisees would affect customers. Franchise owners were having difficulty earning sufficient profit due to expenses imposed on them by corporate Quiznos. Franchisees were forced to buy their restaurant supplies directly from a Quiznos subsidiary, American Food Distributors, at prices that franchisees claimed were inflated. In turn, angry franchisees did not treat their customers very well. In 2006, franchisees launched a class action lawsuit against Quiznos, accusing the company of racketeering and fraud for the rules it imposed on them, resulting in a $206 million settlement in the franchisees' favor. Around the same time, there was a widely reported case where a Quiznos' franchisee took his own life out of anger at the company.

Quiznos' advantage had been offering a "toasted" sandwich peak, until Subway had toasters installed at all its locations, taking away Quiznos' unique advantage. Building a brand on a faulty franchising foundation was a problem, but Quiznos also failed to compete, and to satisfy its customers. (Source #3, 16)

Fred Santino

(Source -FS)

Chapter Four
Coffee and Customers

Starbucks has experienced a significant drop in customer traffic, with a six percent decline in U.S. orders during the fourth fiscal quarter of 2024. This downturn is largely attributed to the increased pricing, which has become a barrier for many regular customers. Economic factors such as inflation and reduced dining out habits are worsening the situation. The need to increase prices was attributed to several factors, including higher costs of ingredients and the recession. Many customers are turning toward cheaper competition, such as gas stations like Cumberland Farms coffee, priced at $1.29.and fast-food chains, like McDonalds McCafe priced at $1.00. Starbucks' struggles reflect consumer fatigue with the rising costs and long wait times. Starbucks had a significant drop in US orders recently. Starbucks customers say that in addition to the rising costs, there are long wait times. More than 30 percent of customers reported waiting as long as 15 minutes for their order, with some even waiting up to half an hour. One former Starbucks customer said he now frequents a local coffee shop with cheaper options, saving him roughly $150 per month.

Fred Santino

Starbucks Revenue – Annual

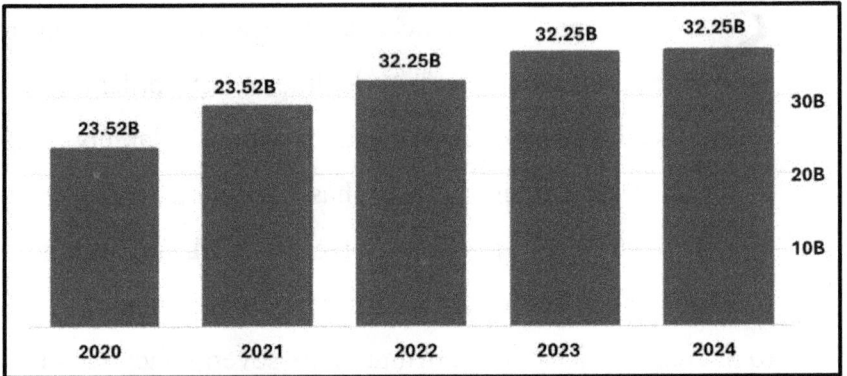

(Source: Stock Analysis, New York, NY)

Market Share of US Coffee Shops

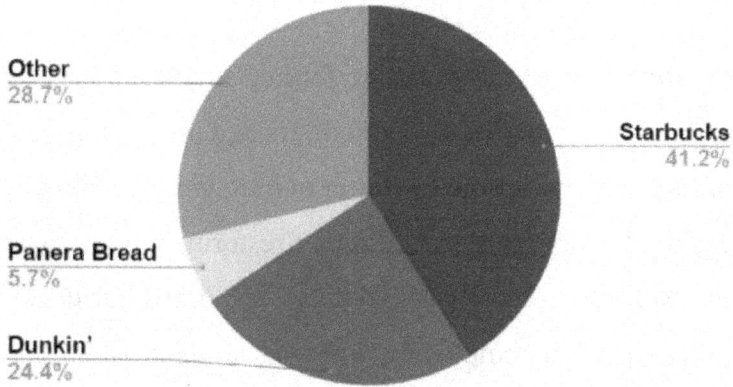

Other
28.7%

Starbucks
41.2%

Panera Bread
5.7%

Dunkin'
24.4%

Even former Starbucks CEO Howard Schultz admitted there was a failure in the mobile ordering system, which is 30 percent of the business. The increase in mobile orders has led to unexpected congestion in stores, particularly around mobile order pickup counters.

Starbucks has tried to entice former customers back to the chain through a flurry of discount offers and promotions, as well as restructuring workflow for faster output, but the company has little wriggle room for the culture firestorm it has repeatedly found itself in. Recently, Starbucks has drawn criticism for allegedly squashing employees' attempts at unionizing.

CEO Laxman Narasimhan left his position in August 2024. Starbucks brought in a new CEO, Brian Niccol, known for his successful turnaround of Chipotle. The company is hoping that Niccol's experience and leadership can rejuvenate the struggling chain and improve its standing and operations amid widespread customer dissatisfaction. In response to the faltering customer visits, Starbucks has launched several promotional strategies. These include BOGO (Buy One, Get One free) days and new food-and-drink combos. Starbucks is also introducing to-go only stores that prioritize quick pick up without offering seating or restroom facilities. This new format is designed to cater to urban customers looking for quick service but shifts away from the traditional coffee shop experience, which was more conducive to relaxing and socializing. These efforts are aimed at maintaining customer interest and lessening the impact of the financial downturn by offering more value for money. The company also introduced new technology to cut down the time it takes to make cold drinks. Faster blenders and new dispensers for ingredients like milk and ice are set up so employees can prepare the beverage without stooping to reach for other ingredients under the counter.

The coffee business largely depends on convenience. Starbucks has multiple locations that make it easy for the customer to patronize. Despite its challenges, Starbucks is still a top-performing US company and has seen market growth since its most disappointing report.

Fred Santino

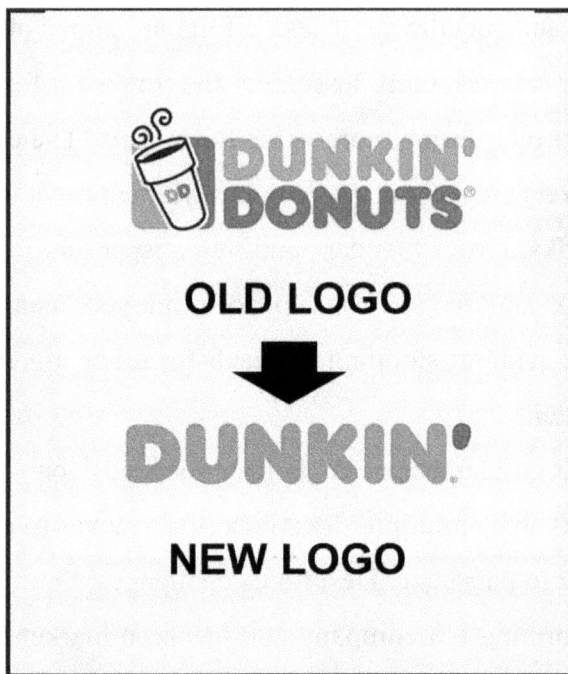

Dunkin changes their name (Dunkin, Inc.)

Dunkin' new fountains (PD)

Dunkin' Are Changes Enough?

Dunkin' Donuts has been facing several challenges, including a shortage of labor where franchisees were unable to find enough employees to run their businesses. Declining retail traffic: retail sales were shifting away from malls and strip malls. Health concerns, including the risks of high sugar consumption may have made it more difficult to sell doughnuts and Munchkins. With the lessened popularity of doughnuts, in January 2019 the chain began rebranding as a "beverage-focused" company." After 68 years of "Dunkin' Donuts" the chain said it wanted people to think of its stores as a destination for coffee and was renamed simply "Dunkin." Stores in the U.S. began using the new name, the company intends to eventually roll out the rebranding to all its international stores. Dunkin' began remodeling its stores to "Next Generation" stores designed for efficiency to shorten customer wait times. Dunkin' created the industry's first mobile-order-only drive-thru lane and separate pickup experience for in-store mobile-order customers. They also installed "bar-like" fountains for quick dispensing of varied beverages.

In 2024, Dunkin' Donuts faced lawsuits, including charging extra for non-dairy milk. A group filed a lawsuit against Dunkin' Donuts for charging more for non-dairy milk, saying that is discrimination against customers who have problems drinking regular milk. A potential class-action lawsuit alleges that

Fred Santino

Next Gen Dunkin' store interior (DD)

Consumer Focused Behavior

Dunkin's operation violates the "Americans with Disabilities Act" because lactose intolerance and milk allergies are both considered disabilities

A former Dunkin' employee gave his comments. "Dunkin' has been around for 74 years, and in that time its customers have built an expectation. That expectation is good, high-quality coffee, fresh donuts, and hot food that's made to order by employees that are happy to serve you." He also said,
"None of the Dunkin' employees know how to properly brew coffee. Dunkin' no longer grinds their beans in the store, the pre-ground coffee is sent to stores in a bag that is poured into an electric grinder that no one knows how to calibrate, then brewed by an electric brewer that no one knows how to calibrate and left to sit there for hours on end until someone orders it. The doughnuts are not fresh. My store received its daily doughnut delivery, made by a contracted bakery somewhere nearby, every night at around 9:00 pm. They would sit there wrapped in plastic overnight until 3:00 am when the baker got there to frost, fill, and place the donuts on trays. Once the Covid pandemic hit the bakers were basically laid off, leaving the shift leads to go in earlier and do everything themselves to offset the loss of revenue that didn't happen because business never dropped." He added, "When an order came in for "sandwich food" (eggs, bacon,

sausage, etc) the sandwich would be put together in about 20 seconds, microwaved, and placed on a counter with no regard to whether the food was still hot or how long it would sit there before it got to the customer. Employees are not happy to serve their many customers. They are overworked, underpaid, and generally mistreated by their employers and customers just like everywhere else. Some places were better than others, but for the most part people generally dislike their jobs there. I could go into more detail, but I will save you all the gore since I think you get the general idea."

That type of candid comment made me think that Dunkin is still in need of major attention.

Next Generation Interior – Dunkin (PD)

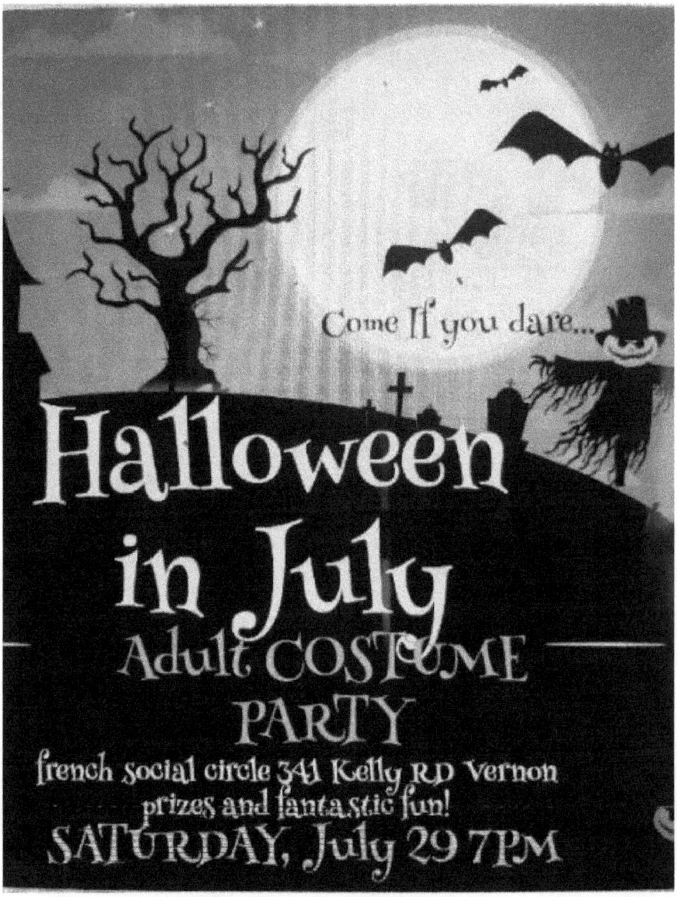

Out of season ad (FS)

Chapter Five
Holiday Promotion

Holiday shopping used to be more of a last-minute errand. Even Christmas, which now has an entire dedicated season, did not get nearly as much early play from retailers In the early 1900s, Christmas shopping was basically done a few days before Christmas. The whole family would gear up to go to that retail area and they would shop for Christmas presents and then they would go home. That began to change over time, he said, especially leading into World War I. There was a push to have people do the shopping earlier to relieve the burden on the supply chain and it just continued since then. Many retailers now rely on the holiday season to account for up to 30 percent of annual sales, creating an incentive to expand the timeline even further. Thanksgiving was traditionally a barrier that limited opportunities for stores to sell holiday-themed goods until December. These days, retailers are looking for opportunities to spread their sales out through more of the year, and to promote their holiday merchandise as early as possible. Are the retailers driving the demand or are they responding to consumer wants and needs?

Fred Santino

As summer drags on, in July and August, most people are traveling to beaches, or local pools, and blasting their air conditioning. Other people are shopping for Halloween items such as large skeletons and scarecrows for their yards, or clothing embossed with ghosts and witches. Some people have called this summertime interest in Halloween "Summerween." Retailers are taking advantage of this early interest in Halloween and making space for Halloween merchandise. Firms such as "Spirit" are opening "pop-up" seasonal Halloween stores in vacant shopping mall locations. Has Halloween always been this way? And when did it become an entire month or even season somewhat reminiscent of Christmas?

Spirit store in Summer, Nashua, NH (FS)

Fred Santino

Home Depot became one of the Halloween icons in 2020 after their twelve-foot skeleton decoration went viral online. Since then, the company has been posting its Halloween collection live on its website in July. Home Depot also began hosting a springtime event somewhat akin to Christmas in July, called the "Halfway to Halloween" sale, giving enthusiasts a chance to buy Halloween items as early as April. Home Depot have seen customers decorating earlier each season for the last five years. Having products available when they want them is important to Home Depot's customers.

Walk into almost any store in July and you are likely to see Halloween, or Christmas merchandise, even as beach merchandise is still on the shelves. Michaels, HomeGoods, Hobby Lobby, Costco Walmart, Target and Lowe's begin displaying items as early as the first week of July. Some of these retailers are offering either early, exclusive online sales or previews.

Christmas in July or August sales are a common promotion now. By mid-to-late August, you may have a hard time finding any retailer that has not put out seasonal merchandise early. Halloween and Christmas seasons have expanded far beyond their original seasons.

When it comes to maximizing seasonal sales, timing is key, retailers have learned. When deciding when to release holiday items, the biggest determining factor is customer demand. Holiday launches are timed to match their customer's needs and growing enthusiasm for early preparation. (Source #24)

Fred Santino

Remote work (PD)

Chapter Six
Remote Work Thrives

Working from home is a relatively new experience. In the early 1990s, when technology and computing began to connect web users worldwide, companies began to embrace remote work as a viable structure for the first time. Cell phones facilitated the idea even more as businesspeople and entrepreneurs handled dealings from their homes, airports, restaurants or anywhere. In 2019, prior to the COVID-19 pandemic, nearly two-thirds of employees said they hardly ever worked from home. Only a small number (about six percent) of employees worked remotely full time, but a larger number of employees did occasional remote work.

In 2020, the pandemic created a situation where everything that was feasible became remote work overnight. Most of these remote employees worked for communications, information technology media, and management. The share of the American workforce working from home more than tripled from 2019 to 2021. The most notable gains were reduced overhead costs and access to a wider pool of talent. For those who switched to working remotely, their employment lives have changed somehow. These days, in many cases, working from home is a decision in the hands of employees. Nearly two-thirds of those who worked from home, but had a workplace elsewhere said they opted not to commute to their job. One of the hardest things about committing to a nine-to-five desk job is that it prevents you from being able to handle almost anything else that comes up in your life, whether it is getting to a medical appointment or picking up an ill child at school. While you still must meet your deadlines and be available when you say you will be, you generally have opportunity to tend to other responsibilities when you work from home. Many say that avoiding traffic is a major benefit of working from home. Employees can save a lot of money – nearly $9,000 a year on average and avoid wasting time commuting. In addition to saving drive time and gas expenses, the work-from-home crowd can generally save on clothing costs. While you may need to have professional attire at the ready for video calls, most employees who work from home have more freedom to wear what they want while they work.

One disadvantage of working from home are less positive review by superiors. You may find that your contributions are not noticed or appreciated. Other disadvantages include distractions, unmonitored performance, lack of motivation, communication and collaboration, increased home office costs, and loneliness, and missing out on office perks.

Consumer Focused Behavior

Remote Work (PD)

Fred Santino

There is less opportunity to interact in person with people at your company. Miscommunication is another disadvantage It is possible to misread cues from impersonal electronic communications. Many remote workers report difficulty getting the tone right when using digital communication systems such as email, chat, social media, text and other platforms. Without body language, facial expressions and other cues, remote employees must put in extra effort to maintain positive communication.

Remote workers must motivate themselves to get the job done, which forces people working from home to manage their time wisely to complete their projects. Some data shows that work-from-home employees have higher levels of satisfaction, improved well-being, and increased engagement. The U.S. Bureau of Labor Statistics found that employers who offer remote work to employees are only half as likely to experience turnover, and those employees have an improved performance of compared to their in-person counterparts. They also found that if workers returned to in-person work environments, productivity decreased by nearly ten percent.

Remote work has proven to be a potent negotiation tool for companies seeking top-tier talent, as remote workers are happier and more productive thanks to the flexibility provided by the work from home structure. Because companies compete to recruit the best talent within their respective industries, many find it increasingly necessary to offer work from home as a benefit. In addition to reducing office costs and transportation fees, employers can also minimize relocation costs as there is less of a need to move employees closer to company headquarters.

The increase in remote work will cause negative effects on other businesses that thrive on supporting traditional office work, Downtown restaurants depend on office workers. Airlines and hotels rely heavily on business travelers. Demand for cars, fuel, and public transit rely on daily commuters. These are all sectors that have been impacted from increased working at home and will likely shrink permanently as more work is done remotely. An important benefit of remote work is that employees have a wider range of possible places to settle without needing to worry about a daily commute.

Doing more remote work typically will require an Internet speed increase, plus hardware and software upgrades. Dated communication systems, collaborative workspaces, security protocols and other technologies will likely need upgrades to meet work goals. Outdated technology can hinder your business's overall operational success and security. (Source #4)

Fred Santino

Disney World (PD)

Chapter Seven
Theme Parks Decline

Faced with rising costs and tight finances, many consumers opted out of summer theme park visits. Drops in theme parks' financial results show that consumers are spending their time and money elsewhere. It may also be a sign that theme parks are not doing enough to attract visitors.

Disney, Universal and Six Flags have all reported lower earnings for their theme parks. Disney revealed that their operating profit had dropped three percent. Universal reported that theme park revenue had decreased by over ten percent. Six Flags reported that revenue had dropped one percent and guest attendance had dropped two percent. Visitors also complained about the amount of time waiting in line at the parks.

According to Disney's information, a trip to Disney World would cost a family of four several thousand dollars. This is competing with other vacation options. When people pay more for mortgages, they have less money for vacations. That is just basic finance, however, costs associated with the parks have also skyrocketed. The base price of an adult ticket increased one-third between 2014 and 2025. The most expensive adult tickets have increased ninety-one percent. The average cost of a Walt Disney World vacation, for a family of four over four days, has increased nearly $1,000 since 2019, "no matter which hotel you stay at," Over seventy percent of this increase comes from costs for things that used to be free, like the airport shuttle to their Disney hotel. The shuttle service was discontinued in 2021 and visitors are now expected to pay to make their own way to their hotels.

Despite lower profits, Disney's earning statement noted that per capita spending had increased slightly. The company acknowledged that the "demand moderation" it has seen recently "could impact the next few quarters." Many travelers could decide that the artificial pleasures of the "happiest place on earth" cannot compare to the potentially life-changing experience of traveling the world. (Source #6)

Consumer Focused Behavior

Disney World ride (FS)

Fred Santino

Vinyl Record Turntable (PD)

Chapter Eight
Vinyl Records in the Digital Age

For most of the 20th century, vinyl records were the only popularly available music format in the US. However, with the introduction of new recorded music formats, each one of which was a "disruptive innovation" that was not "backward compatible" to the previous formats, all that changed.

First came eight-track and cassette tapes in the early 1970's and 1980's. These formats were cheaper, smaller, and could be played in your car, which was a game-changer for many music fans. Next came compact discs (CDs) in the late 1980's, which were smaller than cassettes or records, and allowed you to skip immediately to your favorite songs.

When digital streaming and downloading were introduced in 2004, the vinyl record format had declined to only two-tenths percent of the total sales revenue of all recorded music formats. However, starting in 2007, vinyl record sales began increasing year over year, a trend that is continuing. This development surprised many in the music industry, including manufacturers, vinyl records are experiencing an unexpected renaissance in the digital age. Record Store Day was launched in 2008 to promote independent record stores in the U.S. As part of the annual event, limited numbers of special vinyl and CD releases are made available at participating record stores. The event was so successful that it helped increase the total U.S. vinyl record sales. The event has expanded significantly since 2008.

In 2022, vinyl records officially surpassed CD's as the most popular physical recorded music format for the first time since 1987 (41.3 million units sold vs. 33.4 million units for CD's). In the first half of 2023, vinyl records brought in 72 percent of all non-digital recorded music format revenues in the U.S., surpassing CD's by a wide margin ($632.4 million vs. $236 million).

In 2021, vinyl records enjoyed a 68 percent increase in total sales volume and a 55 percent increase in total sales revenue over 2020 in the US, reaching $1 billion in sales for the first time since 1985. This jump was likely driven by an increased interest in record collecting that occurred during the COVID-19 pandemic as people looked for new hobbies to keep them occupied during lockdowns and quarantines.

American culture has often rediscovered and been inspired by the trends and styles popular during previous decades. In the 2000s, the 1970s and 1980s experienced a cultural revival, which inevitably led to a renewed interest in music from those decades, most of which were released primarily on vinyl.

Consumer Focused Behavior

Many collectors' record collections have significant value. Their inventories across all genres, are considered collector's items, and are hard to find. Collectors often search estate sales, thrift stores, yard and garage sales, and online.

When collectors are asked why they love vinyl records, most feel that vinyl records sound superior to CD's or digital recordings. Also, many album covers are classic art or photography. The liner notes provide fascinating behind-the-scenes stories of popular artists.

There have been several notable impacts resulting from the revival of the vinyl record market. Large record stores like Tower Records and Sam Goody closed in the 1990's and early 2000's. This left only the small, independently owned record stores to carry the vinyl media. Now, renewed interest in vinyl has breathed new life into these independent record stores, such as Newbury Comics, turning them once again into vital community hubs for music culture. Independent record stores that struggled to stay open during the rise of digital music are now thriving and even opening some new stores. Many of these stores offer a variety of vinyl records, CD's, and cassettes. Many stores also sell their records online on websites like eBay, which provides access to collectors in even the most remote locations.

The revival of the vinyl record industry has interested many established artists to re-release their older albums on vinyl. This has resulted in a significantly higher demand for vinyl record production, one that the vinyl record manufacturing industry was not prepared to meet.

Since the late 1980's, record pressing plants across the country and worldwide had been going out of business as other music formats like CD's gained popularity. By 2015, there were only 21 vinyl pressing plants in operation in the U.S. and only 40 worldwide. This left very few factories with the equipment or employees to meet the growing demand in the early 2000's.

The supply chain problems and factory shutdowns that occurred during the COVID-19 pandemic resulted in a massive backlog of orders, lengthy production delays of a year or more in some cases, and frustrated customers. To respond to the increased demand over the past decade, new or expanded U.S. vinyl record pressing plant projects were planned, such as United Record Pressing plant, Nashville, TN, and the Memphis Record Pressing plant, Tennessee.

It is very unusual when an "obsolete" industry revives the way that vinyl records have. It is unclear whether demand for vinyl records will continue, or will the new collectors just move on to the next trend. The established "old-school" record collectors will stay, but it remains to be seen if this revival might last. (Source #7)

Old Record Store (PD)

Fred Santino

Ryanair (PD)

Southwest (PD)

Chapter Nine
Airline Customer Behavior

R yanair, founded in 1984, with headquarters in Dublin, Ireland, is one of the largest low cost airlines in Europe, with 8400 employees, and 1500 flights/day to 28 countries, Ryanair is also the most profitable airline worldwide. Ryanair prides itself on being the ultimate "no-frills airline," being successful pairing low prices with minimum customer service. The low prices bring customers back, because that is what they can afford. Ryanair is also one of the safest airlines, having never suffered a fatality, carrying 1.1 billion passengers. Also, Ryanair has experienced only one near miss.

Ryanair is trying to add more airports and flights to attract more business travelers. To cut costs, Ryanair persuaded airports to lower fees. Recently, Ryanair offered "premium" business service with priority boarding, premium seats and other comforts. Despite attempts to improve customer service and treat customers better, Ryanair is still getting criticized for poor passenger experiences. Customers complain but put up with bad service to get cheap fares. Ryanair advertises low fares, then adds endless fees for everything. Ryanair CEO, Michael O'Leary, even floated the idea of "charging passengers to use the lavatory" and proposed removing toilets to make room for more revenue-generating seats. O'Leary also called his customers "idiots" which angered some, but most customers expected it. "Our bookings are full of passengers who swore they'd never fly with us again." Ryanair was named the worst customer service in the UK, "Staff are rude, unpleasant, aggressive and hostile towards customers," "lost luggage, flight cancellations and problems with tickets."

Ryanair has a high employee turnover. The airline charges employees for training, uniforms, ID badges, in-flight meals and snacks, and doesn't give sick leave or extra pay for holiday or weekend work. In a survey, many Ryanair pilots said that the airline ignores pilots' safety concerns and had no confidence in Ryanair's safety reporting system. Ryanair may have overestimated just how bad an experience customers will tolerate – no matter how low the price. Recently, Ryanair's flight bookings and profits started falling, and has had a hard time competing against the low-cost Hungarian airline WizzAir. An industry focus group found, "Nine of ten people said they'd leave any brand treating them poorly, regardless of price." Ryan Chief Executive, J. Jacobs said that "brands don't need to be loved, they just need to stand out." Dara Brady, a Ryan manager, disagreed saying "People are individuals and consumer behavior is changing." To counter its bad reputation and poor service image, Ryanair said it would try to be "nicer" to customers but continued to receive around 80,000 complaints per year. Ryanair achieved a customer satisfaction score of only 45 percent for 2019, the sixth year in a row that Ryanair placed last. Given a choice of terms to describe the airline, many respondents picked "greedy," "sneaky" and "arrogant". The Telegraph UK, reported that "despite changes,' the in-flight experience was the same, and food is still a rip off."

In 2022, Ryanair convened its first Customer Panel meeting, and launched a suite of radical improvements to its customer service. Ryanair's Director of Marketing, Dara Brady said, "These improvements allow our guests to self-serve online when changing flight dates, passengers' names, contact information or adding bags. They can also receive live status updates online."

In 2024 airline surveys, Ryanair moved up to the second worst airline in the world, with Hungary's WizzAir rated as the number one worst airline. Customers are not necessarily happy, yet the low prices bring them back because price seems the most important for a large sector of the population. Since Ryanair is profitable and meeting customers' expectations, why would they want to change anything? (Source #9)

Fred Santino

Southwest Airlines assigned seating

Southwest Airlines has traditionally had an open seating policy where passengers could choose their own seats after boarding. However, in July 2024, the airline announced that it would be moving to assigned seating, starting next year. The airline said its research showed 80 percent of customers prefer assigned seating Passengers will purchase tickets with assigned seats when they book their flight. The change is intended to reduce stress during the boarding process and make Southwest more like other airlines like American Airlines and United Airlines. Southwest also plans to offer premium seating with more legroom on all flights. Southwest's open seating policy had been in place for over 50 years, unlike every other major airline. Passengers were only assigned a boarding group and a number that represented a reserved spot within that group. Some say the system became less open over time as Southwest allowed people to pay extra to guarantee a spot near the front of the line. However, many Southwest loyalists still love open seating, but Southwest CEO Robert Jordan expressed confidence that the airline can win over those customers. The shift will affect how customers of the discount carrier select seats and board planes. Southwest passengers, including longtime fans of the open seating policy, will also be able to choose different types of seats for a price, including those offering more legroom. These changes could affect ticket costs across the board, according to experts, although Southwest has not addressed pricing or indicated that regular seat costs will change.

Their open seating model was cited as the number one reason passengers opted to fly other airlines. Because of the assigned boarding number, customers know in advance exactly when they will board.

Some people have complained that they always fly with just a carry-on and no checked luggage, in part because they are worried about their bags getting lost. It also means navigating the chaos that can be found at essentially every other airline's gate besides Southwest. With Southwest, the customer does not have to plan to get a good seat on the flight, just to check in on time. Southwest says that it has received a lot of positive feedback from customers on how calm and orderly their boarding process is. Southwest had the fastest boarding process in the industry. For some people, they found it easier than picking seats for everyone in advance. Though many customers may ultimately welcome the change, the open seating has been an integral part of the Southwest brand for over half a century, in addition to its two free check bags and low-cost fare options. Without the open seating, the airline is losing part of what sets it apart, even if that means gaining new customers. For Southwest, it came down to satisfying a broader customer appeal. (Source #10)

Fred Santino

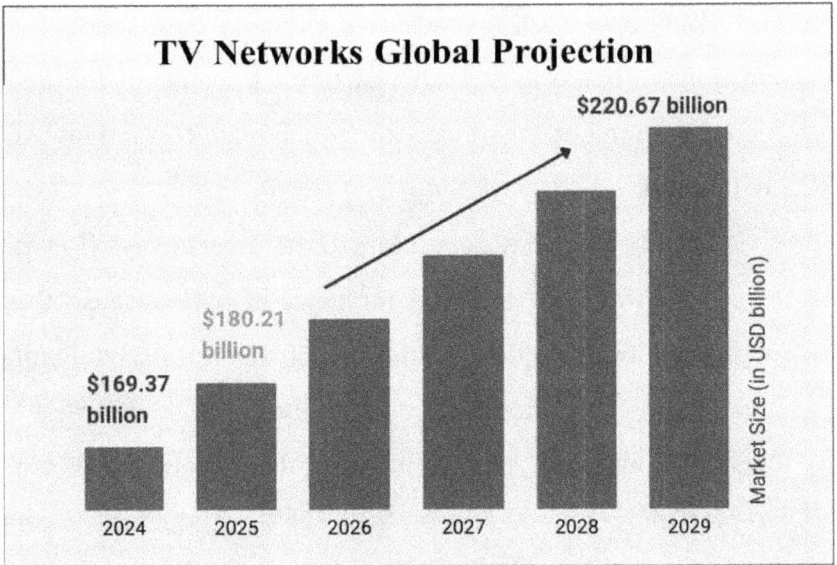

TV Networks Global Projection

$220.67 billion

$180.21 billion

$169.37 billion

Market Size (in USD billion)

2024 2025 2026 2027 2028 2029

(Source: Business Research Corp. New York, NY)

Chapter Ten
Streaming vs. Cable TV

S treaming services have become more popular than cable TV, with streaming services accounting for 40.3 percent of U.S. TV usage in July 2024, compared to 27.2 percent for cable and 20.5 percent for broadcast. This is a significant shift from 2022, when cable and broadcast accounted for 58 percent of TV viewing, while streaming accounted for 32 percent. Streaming has been growing steadily since surpassing cable in July 2022, and 99 percent of U.S. households now subscribe to at least one streaming service.

Streaming first surpassed cable TV in July 2022 and has continued growing steadily since then. The demise of cable TV is coming sooner than expected, due to competition from streaming services. According to Nielsen, this past July, for the first time, TV and cable combined made up less than 50 percent of total viewership, a record low. If any further proof of streaming's leading role in today's television landscape was needed, then here it is: According to Nielsen, streaming services reached a record share of 40.3 percent of TV usage in the United States. Streaming is usually cheaper, but you may have to buy several streaming services to receive all the content that you want.

Streaming requires a stable and reasonably fast internet connection. If your internet is slow or unreliable, you may experience buffering, lower video quality, or interruptions while streaming. While some streaming platforms offer free versions with ads, many require a subscription fee.

The streaming service industry is being led by Netflix, Disney, and Amazon. In 2007 Netflix changed its business model from being a mail-in DVD service to an online platform that gave viewers immediate access to its list of movies at their viewing pleasure.

Looking back, the rise of the streaming service industry started with YouTube, before its acquisition by Google. While the company did not stream TV shows or movies, its business platform is what ultimately drove Netflix to change from a mail-to-home service to a streaming service. Several key factors allowed streaming services to prosper. Streaming services were more affordable, gave viewers access to more shows and movies at one time, avoided advertisements, and allowed watchers to enjoy from anywhere on any platform, all categories that cable TV could not compete with. Viewers could watch their favorite titles at any time they wanted. This led to the 'binge' movement where viewers could start and finish entire shows within a week's time. Viewers could watch their favorite shows at will without having to worry about recording ahead of time.

As we entered the 2020's, subscription-based streaming services became incredibly competitive. Once dominated by Netflix, the market saw increased competition bringing more variety in the TV shows and movie titles offered across providers. However, with increased competition, more companies fought over the rights to the most popular shows and movies. This left most households with no option but to purchase a subscription plan with one or more of these companies. In 2015, only 50 percent of U.S. households held subscriptions to streaming services, but this has grown to 83 percent in 2023.

Because of high competition, streaming service companies turned to produce original content. Amazon Prime Video, Netflix, and Apple+ led the way, and started casting, directing, and filming their own shows and movies. The second alternative to producing original content was the acquisition of competing companies. Companies in the streaming service industry have found buying out the competition to be one of the cheapest options. For example, Disney bought the majority share in Hulu from Comcast, giving Disney full control in late 2023, in a deal valued at $8.6 billion. Other deals have included the Paramount merger with Skydance and Disney's acquisition of 21st Century Fox.

which did boost their subscriber count but frustrated many viewers. The second solution was ad-supported subscription options. Hulu was a pioneer in this field for a long time. Since the 2010's, Hulu always offered an ad-supported option, which saw a lot of success. In fact, in 2020, the ad-supported plan was so successful that Hulu decreased the monthly subscription from $7.00 to $5.00. However, as streaming services began to see decreases in revenue growth, they turned to ad-supported plans, not as an affordable option for consumers, but as a way of increasing their revenues. Almost everything that once made streaming services so desirable over cable TV disappeared as streaming companies did all they could to boost their profits.

It is not clear what the future will bring for the streaming service industry. Many market "experts" estimate the industry to continue to trend upwards in the upcoming years, but if viewers continue to become disappointed by higher prices and more ads the growth may decline. Customers may return to traditional cable subscriptions. If service providers see negative profits, they may have to sell off assets.

Innovation may bring some new ways of providing content, disrupting the market, and rendering present services obsolete. Consumers and industry should be ready for change. (Source #11)

Chapter Eleven
Online Shopping

Ecommerce has caused consumer behavior to change drastically over the last few years. While physical on-site shopping was once the primary way to shop, online shopping was already becoming a favored way to shop for consumers around the globe and this accelerated during the Covid-19 pandemic.

Amazon shopper (PD)

Amazon Prime delivery (PD)

Fred Santino

As of January 2024, 97.1 percent of the US population, or about 331.1 million people, had access to the internet. As of April 2024, 79 percent of the US population shops online, with 41 percent of Americans shopping online at least once a week. This number is expected to increase to almost 285 million shoppers in 2025. Advances in ecommerce are the driving factors behind this shopping evolution. Consumers no longer need to go out to shop and no longer must wait until store hours to make a purchase. Desktop and mobile devices have brought the shopping to them. This completely changed the way consumers shop. The line between online and offline shopping has been blurred. Consumers can shop from anywhere, anytime, having a big impact on consumer shopping habits. Mobile has taken ecommerce to the next level because shoppers can use the device at any point during the sales cycle, including discovering new products, locating products, and comparing prices. By 2025, mobile commerce sales are projected to reach $728.28 billion and make up 44.2 percent of retail commerce sales in the U.S. Rather than having two distinct channels, both channels can be used in conjunction to optimize the shopping experience. Though some of the legacy brick-and-mortar brands initially had trouble with the growth of ecommerce, most have been able to make the transition by creating apps and started selling products through their social media channels. By doing this, they have given consumers the choice of where, when, and how to shop. A shopper can purchase a product online at midnight, receive it the next day, and then return it to a physical store if unhappy with the product. That's the power of mobile ecommerce, the ability to create a more seamless, omnichannel shopping experience.

The progression of ecommerce has advanced the customer expectations of the companies they buy from. Customers now expect a seamless shopping experience that is personalized to them, one that is consistent no matter what device they are using for their shopping or what stage of the buying process. In addition, people are 40 percent more likely to buy if their experience is personalized. The challenge for retailers is they have to offer better experiences than they have in the past to motivate customers to come in or make a purchase. Companies are doing this by creating omnichannel, personalized experiences with content that "resonates, engages and delights consumers" at every stage of the buying process. When companies create a great shopping experience, people want to share that experience with others. Digital marketing has facilitated that sharing and turned shopping into a social activity. What's more, consumers today rely on the opinions of others to guide their purchase decisions, and they have immediate access to those reviews. Anyone on social media can be an influencer for a brand. Social platforms and online review sites have opened the floodgates for word-of-mouth advertising via product reviews. Today, 95 percent of shoppers read reviews before making a purchase. And it does not matter to consumers that these reviews are from complete strangers. They trust the reviews more than they trust what brands themselves are saying. That is why, consumers, not brands, are more responsible now for shaping the perception of a brand. These online reviews have become so important that 94 percent of people have avoided a business because of a negative online review, the company's research shows. Retailers have recognized the power of these channels to shape shoppers' opinions and have begun engaging with their customers on social media and online review platforms. Social media has played a big role in providing customers with information before making purchases. Consumers are more informed than ever before about the products they are buying and the companies they are doing business with.

Shoppers are becoming their own salespeople. In addition to online reviews, consumers can access product and company information that they can read and analyze before buying. These better-informed customers are changing the role of salespeople in companies. These customers' expectations are higher, and companies are having to change their approach to meet those expectations. Before digital media, customers relied on salespeople to guide them on their path to making the best

Consumer Focused Behavior

purchase. Now customers enter stores, online and offline, armed with the information they need to make a purchase.

Today's consumers have access to more information, and ecommerce has given them access to products from around the world. New trade agreements and advances in ecommerce technology has opened the door for brands to sell outside their domestic markets and customers are bought in.

The evolution continues. Customers want products timely and at reasonable prices. Ecommerce gives consumers access to information, shop on different devices and to share their experiences with others, which has completely altered their expectations and the way they shop. Customer shopping habits will continue to evolve with technology, and companies will have to continue to adapt to consumer behavior. (Source #21)

Fred Santino

Instagram

NETFLIX

TikTok

Chapter Twelve
Social Media and Consumers

Consumer behavior is changing with the increasing interactions of consumers on social media. In today's technology-driven environment, businesses that grasp the intricacies of consumer behavior have a competitive edge. They are better able to innovate in product development and align offerings with consumer preferences. The boundaries between social media and e-commerce are increasingly blurred, with social commerce emerging as a force reshaping the retail market. Social commerce is not just a passing fancy, but a response to changing consumer behavior. This is a response to evolving consumer behaviors. This year, U.S. adults are expected to spend about 11 percent of their total daily media time and 18 percent of their digital media time on social platforms. Driven by the considerable time consumers spend on social media, social commerce presents an opportunity to potentially drive revenue by interacting on platforms like TikTok, Facebook, and Instagram. Social commerce integrates social media with the convenience of e-commerce. It allows for the direct purchase of products within a social platform, streamlining the customer experience by eliminating the need to switch platforms. This integration offers consumers a seamless transaction from product discovery to purchase. Social commerce thrives on creating demand for products that consumers might not have been actively sought, particularly discretionary items, such as fashion and beauty products. A 2023 forecast reveals a diverse demographic: 23 percent of U.S. online shoppers are aged 25-34 and 67 percent are under age 44. Platforms like Instagram, Facebook, and TikTok have substantial engagement from this demographic category. A significant portion of the shopping by of younger shoppers is heavily influenced by influencer endorsements and peer reviews. Facebook, Instagram, and TikTok offer digital storefronts features like Facebook Marketplace, Instagram Shopping, and TikTok Shop. Social commerce sales are expected to increase into the future. Despite rapid growth, social commerce faces consumer concerns about data privacy and the authenticity of products. Marketers are encouraged to explore innovative strategies like user-generated content and influencer marketing to connect with consumers and drive sales. Brands must continue to adapt and innovate to thrive in this market to convert interactions into sales directly within social platforms.

An influencer's endorsements and authentic reviews on social media can heavily influence purchasing decisions. Marketers can collaborate with influencers to promote their products with the influencer's dedicated and engaged audience.

Consumer Focused Behavior

In 2022, the median salary for social media influencers in the United States was $45,406, with the lowest earners making around $29,349 and the highest earners making around $72,654. How much influencers earn varies depending on several factors, including their follower count, engagement, and the type of content they create: Influencers with more followers generally earn more per post. Influencers with 1,000–10,000 followers might earn $50–$300 per post, while influencers with over 1 million followers might earn $10,000 or more per post.

Consumers use social media to share their experiences with products and services. These reviews and feedback are valuable resources for potential buyers, influencing their choices. The marketer can engage with customers by responding to their queries and complaints on social media and addressing comments posted. This proactive approach improves a brand's reputation by building a positive perception among both existing and potential customers. The integration of social media and e-commerce has had a powerful effect on brands and has proven to be a successful marketing approach. (Source #17)

Fred Santino

Hotel window (PD)

Chapter Thirteen
Hotels and Consumer Behavior

In recent years consumer behavior in the hospitality industry has changed dramatically. Today's travelers are extremely discerning in their choices of hotel properties, and how they book them. Meanwhile, hotels are under pressure to maximize occupancy, fight for every customer and earn their loyalty. Simply relying on traditional marketing practices, offering a promotion or two, or counting on online travel agencies to fill rooms is not enough anymore. The hotel marketplace is different now. The hotel industry must adapt its strategies in line with emerging industry trends to remain profitable. Consumers' increased use of social media has created both challenges and opportunities for hotels, as they determine how to adapt their strategy to respond. Social media has made a huge impact on the tourism industry. Consumers engage with social networking sites to research trips, make informed decisions about their travels and share their personal experiences of a particular hotel, restaurant or airline. TripAdvisor has had a wide-reaching effect on the industry. It has 50 million unique monthly visitors who actively seek travel information and advice from other tourists.

Consumers are dividing into groups based upon their special interests and behavior. In this era of the customer in control, this becomes more pronounced as customers demand travel experiences tailored to the changes in their behaviors and desires as consumers.

Social networking sites like Facebook provide a forum to share travel stories and photos. Review sites like TripAdvisor offer customer opinions, ratings, reviews and comparisons of hotel visits. Today's traveler prefers to stay at a hotel with favorable guest reviews and ratings To be successful, hotels need to modify their facilities and practices to respond to bad reviews and keep up the needs and wants of each generation.

With millennials in the U.S. on track to spend $1.4 trillion each year, travel brands cannot afford to overlook this lucrative market. Many hotel brands are revisiting their hospitality marketing strategies, which have been geared toward traditional travelers. Marketing to millennials demands a unique approach. Many brands built their reputations on providing the same, expected experience at every location around the world. This may have met the conventional needs of older travel markets, but it is completely at odds with freethinking, novelty-seeking millennials. Hotel brands are seeing they must redefine their experience to appeal to the millennial market to earn their business and loyalty. With millennials making up more and more of the travel market, hospitality marketing experts need to appeal to their preferences to bring in their business. All major hospitality brands seem to be responding to millennials' needs. Millennials travel often, taking an average of five business trips each year and extending them into leisure vacations. This audience is more likely to travel abroad than their older counterparts. While the "baby boomer" market primarily wants familiarity, safety, and comfort, millennials are seeking more. Millennials want to experience local culture and are open to exploration, sharing stories about their vacations, and want hotels to provide a unique experience. Millennials are very cost conscious and seek the best deals and promotions. Millennials' travel decisions are often based on the recommendations of friends and family via social media, Travel decisions are often made spontaneously or at the last minute. Many avoid traditional travel agents in favor of planning trips on their mobile devices. Millennials' dependence on digital devices affects every part of their lives, including how they plan, record, and share their travel experiences. Hotels hoping to compete with less expensive accommodations must find a way to connect with millennials. Loyalty programs may be the edge they need. Millennials seem to appreciate the smallest perks, even a free glass of wine or a personal training session in the hotel fitness center. Along with developing the right hospitality marketing message, they need to deliver their message on the right social media to reach the target audience. Travel brands need to maintain a strong online presence and constantly monitor their social media to engage the many millennials who rely on those channels for most of their communication.

Marriott Hotels, like many hotel brands are adding new features and services that appeal to millennial tastes. Marriott says that millennials comprise up to 50 percent of its guests. The traditional hotel brand is innovating to attract younger travelers. Marriott's market research discovered that millennials like travel brands to have strong local connections, provide experiences unique to locations, and offer a sense of community. Marriott encouraged its properties to give guests a taste of the local culture and community. Marriott's Phoenix, Arizona location created a restaurant focusing on local food producers, local craft beer makers, and small wineries. The restaurant provides a unique experience that appeals to millennial interests.

To thrive in today's travel marketplace, hotels must understand travel industry trends that are influencing customers. That means finding what travelers want, watching competitors, and anticipating disruptive trends and technologies. Today's travelers have a whole new set of wants and needs, and consumer behavior continues to change very quickly. (Source #19)

Chapter Fourteen
Adapting to Local Consumers

Many attempts of businesses to expand internationally have failed due to a lack of understanding of the consumer behavioral differences between shoppers of different countries. Tesco, based in Britain, is one of the world's largest retailers, trailing only Walmart and France's Carrefour. Tesco attempted to expand its operations into the United States and failed. The principal reason for Tesco's failure was a failure to understand the American consumer.

Fresh and Easy store closing (PD)

Fred Santino

Tesco first opened in London in 1919. The company started with groceries, then moved into non-food, general merchandise retailing. Currently, Tesco employs over 500,000 people, and has over 100 million total square feet of retail space.

Tesco had spent years considering a move into the U.S. market. With Tesco's resources and initiative, it was only a matter of time before the company attempted to expand into the U.S. market. The company even did two years of focused research, during which they sent senior executives to live in California to observe the consumer behavior of typical U.S. families and the way they shopped and consumed. Tesco assumed that its British model would be successful in the U.S., but this was not the case. American consumers have different shopping habits and preferences than British consumers. American consumers tend to shop for groceries less frequently than British consumers. This is because American households are larger, and they tend to have more cars. As a result, American consumers need to buy more groceries at one time, and they do not need to shop as often. Americans also value service as part of the shopping experience. They expect to be greeted by friendly employees, and they expect to be able to get help quickly if they need it.

In the case of Britain and the U.S., speaking the same language, listening to the same music, and watching the same films is not enough. Other tastes and habits can differ quite dramatically between the two countries. British retail brands have much higher levels of loyalty and have a "one-stop shop" concept. In 2007, Tesco made a two billion commitment to its goal of opening 1,000 U.S. stores in the first five years. Tesco then ignored much of their research, deciding to set up the stores without listening to its potential customers. Tesco rejected the "one-stop supercenter" approach. Instead, Fresh & Easy was designed as a smaller "neighborhood style" store positioned between convenience stores and full-sized supermarkets. Tesco called this an "express" mini supermarket. The average size of a Fresh & Easy Neighborhood Market is 15,000 square feet, compared to a full-sized supermarket at 50,000 to 60,000 square feet.

Tesco failed to understand the American consumer behavior. Tesco's Fresh & Easy stores were intended to be convenient, one-stop-shop stores, but they were not what enough Americans were looking for. The stores were small and offered a limited range of products, which did not appeal to American consumers who were used to larger stores with more extensive product offerings. The American retail market is highly competitive, and consumers have a wide range of options available to them. Tesco's stores did not adapt to the differences in the U.S. Although U.S. shoppers prefer to buy in bulk to save money, Fresh & Easy offered small pack sizes. The stores also stocked British-style ready meals unfamiliar to U.S. shoppers. Tesco's stores in the U.S. were not always staffed with enough employees, and they did not always have the products that American consumers were looking for. Tesco relied heavily on self-service counters. This was unappealing to American customers, who had a high priority for good service. Also, Tesco initially set prices too high for price-sensitive American consumers. Fresh & Easy seemed to miss the mark on meeting the basic consumer needs of their typical customer. A disappointed customer asked why anyone would want to shop here, and said she preferred to shop at Trader Joe's which has more of the items that she typically needed.

In the years before Tesco's 2007 attempt, the U.S. economy was doing well, with new homes being built everywhere. Those new homes and people needed retailers to feed them. As it looked to Tesco, their timing was perfect. Tesco entered the market at the wrong time. Shortly after Tesco's entering the U.S., a global financial crisis caused many consumers to cut back on spending, including on groceries. This made it difficult for Tesco to gain a foothold in the market, as consumers were not interested in trying out new stores or brands. Fresh & Easy's upscale "heat-and-eat" dinners were never going to be top of the weekly shopping list for U.S. families struggling to pay their mortgages and keep their jobs.

Consumer Focused Behavior

Even though Tesco invested over $1.5 billion to establish U.S. stores and a supply chain, the company did not accomplish sufficient market research or adjust its business model to suit the U.S. market. This led to issues with supply chain management and pricing. Tesco also attempted to open too many stores too quickly. This led to inventory management problems, as Tesco was unable to sell enough products to meet its high inventory levels. Tesco did not have sufficient knowledge of consumer markets to find appropriate locations for new stores. They even opened some of its "upscale" grocery stores in areas with too low an average income. Tesco had planned to open several hundred small stores very quickly, because it needed 500 outlets to justify its investment in a U.S. food preparation warehouse. As sales stumbled at the first Fresh & Easy branches, Tesco had to invest money in improving existing stores rather than opening new ones.

The company also struggled to maintain consistency across its stores, with some locations performing better than others. As profits from home were poured into the U.S. business, investment in British stores was put on hold, causing many of the UK stores to deteriorate, and service levels to slide. This negatively affected brand's image in the UK.

Other businesses may think twice before trying to break into any new market, unless they have a complete knowledge of the consumer behavior associated with that market. Tesco's experience serves as a reminder of the importance of conducting thorough market research, adapting business models to suit local markets, and managing supply chains and inventory levels to meet consumer demand. While Tesco may have failed in the U.S., the company remains a successful global retailer. This shows that even the most successful companies can learn from their failures and must adapt their strategies accordingly. (Source #20)

Chapter Fifteen
Retail Customer Service

Consumers in current times want quality, value, convenience, and a trouble-free shopping experience. Retailers need to keep aware of the latest trends in consumer preferences and shopping habits. Businesses that can meet consumer expectations will have a better chance to succeed.

Nordstrom, a large Seattle-based retailer, constantly seeks ways to enhance the customer experience and operational effectiveness. Nordstrom has one main goal: "To provide outstanding service every day, one customer at a time." Nordstrom has been providing superior customer experience ever since 1901 when John Nordstrom and a friend, Carl F. Wallin, opened the Wallin & Nordstrom shoe store, funded by $15,000 from an Alaskan Gold Rush claim. What began as a shoe retailer is now a publicly traded company selling clothing, accessories, handbags, jewelry, cosmetics, and fragrances. Today, more than 365 stores operate in 40 US states, Puerto Rico, and Canada.

According to Nordstrom, they want "employees to consistently connect with customers." And must "treat each customer as an individual, to learn their preferences." Nordstrom wants its employees to create an authentic relationship with customers, so that customers feel they are being served by friends. This approach creates happy customers who may even become "brand influencers."

Nordstrom prioritizes the entire personnel function, including hiring and training processes to find, screen, hire the right people, and then train them. Nordstrom trains employees to empower them to support their customers, rather than micromanaging every situation. Nordstrom fosters a positive workplace culture and ensures that its employees are equipped with the skills and resources they need to excel in their roles. This, in turn, translates into enhanced customer satisfaction and loyalty, as employees who feel valued and supported are more likely to go above and beyond to meet customer needs. They encourage employees to take creative action to solve issues without consulting their supervisor, or a predetermined set of policies. Norstrom's policy is. "Use your best judgment in all situations."

Nordstrom encourages a culture where employees are empowered to identify areas for improvement and implement innovative solutions. By fostering an environment of continuous improvement, Nordstrom stays ahead of evolving customer expectations and market trends. Such a commitment to ongoing enhancement keeps Nordstrom's position as a leader in the retail industry and reinforces its reputation for delivering exceptional service. For Nordstrom, this allows them to get the most out of their employees, while providing greater employee satisfaction

Nordstrom adapts to its customers' wants and needs to ensure that the Nordstrom system benefits the customer because the customer drives the business. A retired Nordstrom executive said, "Selling clothes isn't what we do…it is filling all of people's needs and making them feel better emotionally." Nordstrom tries to personalize the customer experience. When a customer shops at Nordstrom, a personal shopper can help you select clothes that will work with you, as well as avoiding brands, colors, and combinations that are not appropriate for you. Nordstrom makes the experience personal by sending marketing messages, with actual employees' first names. The authentic, personalized email messages support Nordstrom's outstanding customer service.

Nordstrom is known to be an upscale, high-priced store. Despite a "pricey" image, it is surprising that Nordstrom can be so successful. Customers feel that Nordstrom provides a pleasurable and personal experience. The better the customer's experience, the more that price considerations fade away rather than being the central consideration. The quality of the customers' experience helps to minimize price as a consideration.

Nordstrom uses technology to streamline the customer experience. Nordstrom has a "technology team" dedicated to streamlining the customers' shopping experience. Nordstrom wants to be as efficient as the best strictly online companies. Nordstrom recognizes that online customers do not have to wait in line to pay, so they provide customers in the physical store with the same opportunity to pay with their phone. Another example of Nordstrom's use of technology is their shoe sizing technology which can match a customer to the perfect shoe without the need to try on shoes. Applying technology to its customer service provides Nordstrom with a competitive advantage.

In customer service surveys, Nordstrom continually ranks the highest of any company in the consumer fashion retail industry. Good customer service apparently, pays off for Nordstrom. They are said to have the highest sales per square foot performance in the retail industry.

During the recent negative economic situation, many retailers are having difficulty. Nordstrom's stores have been sliding, but they are not doing as badly as some of its competitors. Because of inflation, shoppers must pay more for food and necessities shoppers, so they are seeking deals for other products. Nordstrom has opened "Nordstrom Rack" off-price stores, where customers can find quality merchandise at more affordable prices. Since the end of the Covid-19 pandemic workers has returned to the office and want to be appropriately attired.

Consumer Focused Behavior

Because of Nordstrom's relatively high prices, they are vulnerable to competition from lower-priced retailers, One of Nordstrom's competitors is Macy's, which offers a wider variety of goods, accommodates a wider range of spending ranges and preferences, and more affordable prices than Nordstrom's. Macy's has excellent quality and outstanding customer service, but below the "premium" level of Nordstrom. Some customers will be attracted to Macy's, because of their own price limitations, and Macy's lower price range. However, Nordstrom's premium level of customer service helps them survive.

We can compare the success of Nordstrom with the failure of another large retailer, namely Sears. Shortly after the turn of century, America's largest catalog retailer, made an extraordinary shift. After years of only mailing goods to home shoppers, Sears started operating dozens of physical stores throughout the US, with a model of operational efficiency, technology, strategy, low prices, and customer service.

The company began to introduce its own brands in the 1920s, including Craftsman, DieHard, and Kenmore. It began selling insurance through its Allstate subsidiary in 1931. Sears stores were way ahead of its peers for years. By the 1960's, Sears had 700 stores. In the middle of the 20th century, Sears accounted for a full percentage point of U.S. GDP. In 1969, Sears, the largest retailer in the world, began construction on the world's tallest skyscraper. The Sears' Tower's completion four years marked the company's peak, but its retail dominance began to fade around that time. By the early 21st century, it was in steep decline. What happened? Sears focused on expanding outside retail, and it affected their stores. Sears failed to adjust in the 1970s and 1980s to the decline of manufacturing, and manufacturing jobs, hitting blue-collar families, its most devoted consumers and the value of its real estate near steel towns. In the 1980s, it expanded into financial services, a stockbroker, Dean Witter Reynolds and Coldwell, Banker & Co., a real estate broker. It also launched Discover Card through Dean Witter in 1985. Instead of investing in their brand, Sears cut their marketing budget, relying mainly on minor celebrities to attract younger, fashion-conscious consumers." Sears' targeted advertising was completely ineffective. Sears started going further downhill in 2009 after the introduction of a loyalty program which was confusing and poorly executed, slowing down customer service.

In earlier times, when Sears had a commission-based pay scale and benefits, employees had a strong financial incentive to produce sales. If an employee did not sell, they did not make a living. Around the end of the twentieth century, Sears changed its pay scale and benefits. Sears was not compensating or training people to move their products. Sears cut the hours, pay, and headcount of retail staff to save cash, causing stores and customer experience to deteriorate. in the mid-2000's, other big-box retailers, particularly Walmart, were thriving.

Sears complaints about appliance service and deliveries was exploding out of control. Customers were increasingly finding that in-store customer service was largely nonexistent or overwhelmed. In 2011, the year Sears lost over $3.1 billion, Walmart made $16.4 billion. Sears was giving shoppers even fewer reasons to go to its stores.

According to Neil Saunders, Managing Director of Global Data Retail, "The decline of Sears is not just a reflection of the company's management or competitive challenges, it is a failure to adapt to changing consumer preferences."

Also, I feel that Sears slashed in-store costs despite how much those cuts negatively affected customers. Unhappy customers made it difficult for the company to remain competitive. As of June 2024, there are only thirteen Sears stores left in the United States.

While customer service is obviously important at retailers, the same concepts are equally important to other businesses, such as hospitality, construction, banking, or technology, to achieve success. Poor customer service will provide the opposite result. (Sources #22, 23)

Fred Santino

Epilogue

Consumer behavior, as well as needs, preferences, and the world around, are very susceptible to change over time. The successful business will constantly update its behavior and marketing approaches to be "consumer focused." Hopefully, the case studies in this book will be helpful for businesses to adopt the best practices that contribute to success and customer satisfaction and avoid making the wrong decisions.

Fred Santino

Sources

1. Toyota bets on hybrids, J. Ochoa, TheStreet, Aug 14, 2024
2. Detroit killed sedans, D. Zipper, Fast Co., May13, 2024
3. Subway sales plummet, J. Kosman, NY Post, Aug 2024
4. US Bureau Labor Statistics, Remote Work, May 10, 2024
5. Panera Bread, Amy Bell, Mashed, March 31, 2024
6. Theme parks decline, I. Saric, Axios, Aug 2024
7. Vinyl Records, Ben Sisario, NY Times, Oct. 21, 2021
8. Fed-up at Starbucks, K. Donlevy, NY Post, Aug. 2024
9. Ryanair rated worst, BBC, August 2019
10. Southwest seating, K. Vlamis, Insider, July 2024
11. Streaming, Michigan Journal Economics, May 2024
12. Sweetgreen, Amy Farley, Fast Company, January 2021
13. L. Schiffman. Consumer Behavior, 12e, Pearson, 2019
14. Buyology, M. Lindstrom, Doubleday, 2008
15. M. Solomon, Consumer Behavior, 13e, Pearson, 2023
16. Quiznos Collapse, J. Maze, Restaurant Bus, Jun 2024
17. Influencers In Media, Kat Shee, Forbes, June 2024
18. Panera Menu, J. Fantozzi, Restaurant News, March 2024
19. Hotels target millennials, Alex Blair, Yahoo, July 2024
20. Tesco Failure, S. Butler, The Guardian UK, Dec 2023
21. Online shopping, J. Goldberg, Forbes, Feb 2022
22. Nordstrom's success, Saskia Tillers, CEO, June 28, 2023
23. Demise of Sears, D. Lazarus, LA Times, June 22, 2021
24. Halloween shopping, Sheryll Poe, NRF, October 2023
25. Wikipedia- Consumer Behavior
26. Pixabay.com, Public Domain Images
NOTE: Photos with (FS) sources are the authors own.
Photos with (PD) are public domain.

Fred Santino

About the Author

Fred Santino has been teaching management, technology, and marketing at Boston University for 20 years. He previously taught at Babson College for five years. He also developed new curricula for two community colleges. Besides his teaching, Santino was a Project Engineer with the Electronic Systems Center, where he managed development and implementation of aircraft and communications systems, including "breakthrough" technology. He began his professional career as a marketing intern. Santino has doctoral study in management of technology, and has an M.S. in Engineering Management, and B.S. degrees in both Engineering and Business Administration. Earlier in his career, he deployed twice to the Antarctic with the U.S. Navy, as an avionics technician and aircrew member. He also served as a C-1A Plane Captain in "Carrier on Board Delivery" operations on the aircraft carrier USS Intrepid during the Vietnam War, and on the USS Wasp for NASA spacecraft recovery at sea. Santino enjoys ballroom dancing, performing in musical theatre, and singing, solo, and in a group.

Fred Santino